HOMEWORK HELPERS

Spelling Sticker Book

Written by Amanda Archer
Illustrated by Ian Cunliffe
Educational Consultant: Geraldine Taylor

The journey from A to Z

Every word is made up of letters from the **alphabet**.
The alphabet has 26 letters.

 **Aa**  **Bb**  **Cc**  **Dd**  **Ee**

 **Ff** 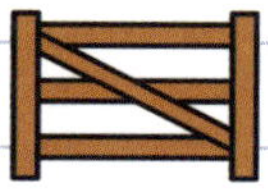 **Gg**  **Hh**  **Ii**  **Jj**

 **Kk**  **Ll**  **Mm**  **Nn** 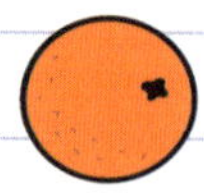 **Oo**

 **Pp**  **Qq**  **Rr** 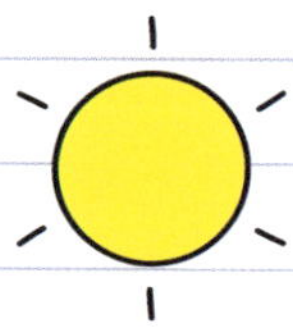 **Ss**  **Tt**

 **Uu**  **Vv**  **Ww**  **Xx** 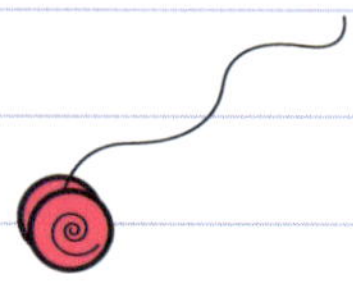 **Yy**  **Zz**

Let's get started!

Find the missing letter stickers to start these words.

ap

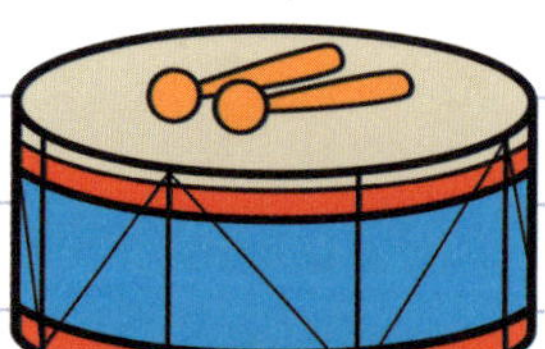
rum

lock

pider

Happy endings

Finish the words in this beach scene by writing in the last letters.

1. boa_

2. umbrell_

3. cra_

4. shel_

5. octopu_

6. starfis_

Letter types

Five letters of the alphabet are called **vowels**.

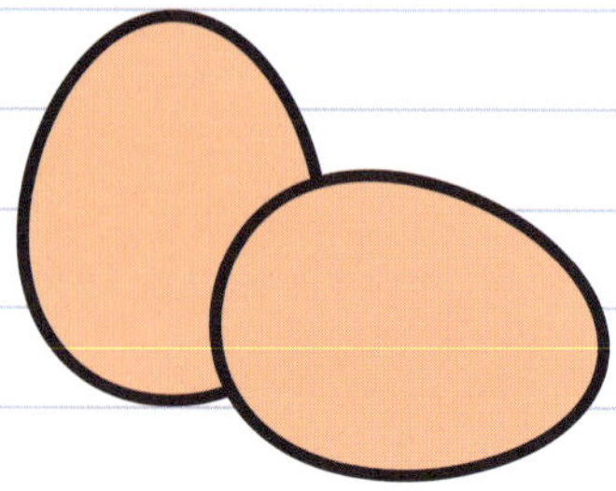

Aa

Ee

Ii

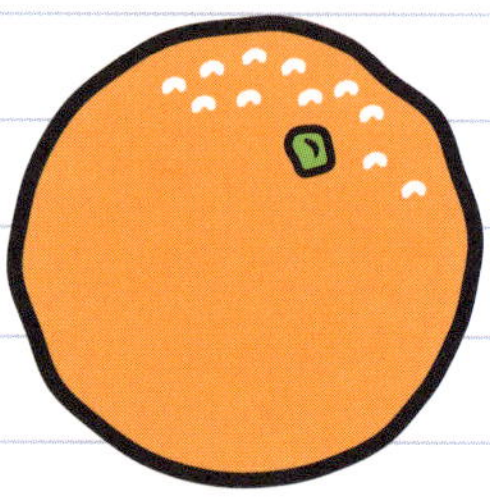

Oo

Uu

The rest are called **consonants**.

Jungle japes

Stick the missing letters onto this curly alphabet snake.

Short and sweet

Short vowel sounds don't take long to say!

Write **a** or **e** to complete these words.

c_t

b_d

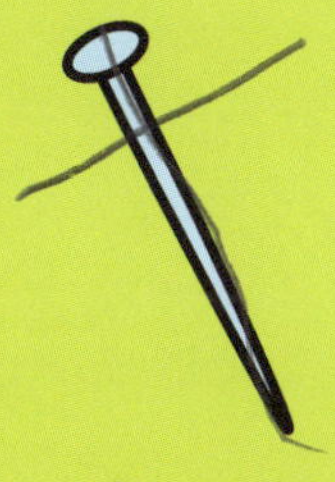

Write **i** or **o** to complete these words.

p_n

f_x

Write **u** or **e** to complete these words.

s_n

p_g

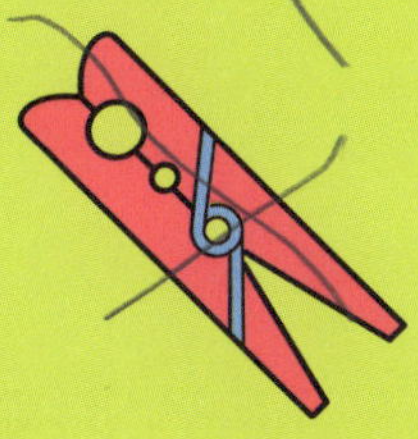

These words all have short vowel sounds.

A little longer

These words have **long** vowel sounds – can you hear the difference between short and long vowels?

Add the right vowel to complete these words.

b_e

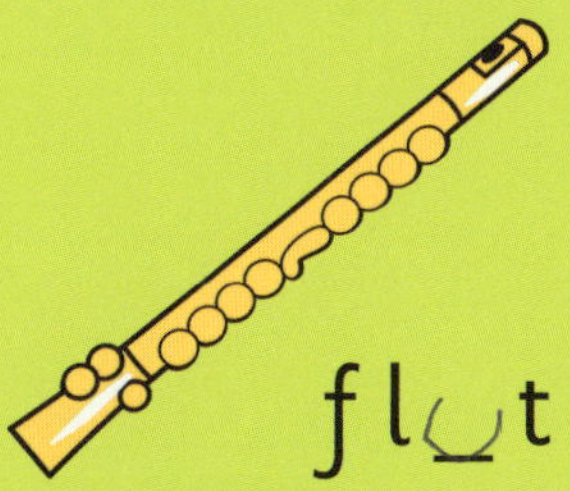

fl_te

k_te

Lots of plurals

A **plural** means 'more than one thing'. We make most nouns plural by adding **s** to the end of the word. Add a sticker to make each word more than one.

apple s

cup s

When a noun ends in **s, x, sh** or **ch** we make it plural by adding **es** to the end. Add a sticker to make each word plural.

box es

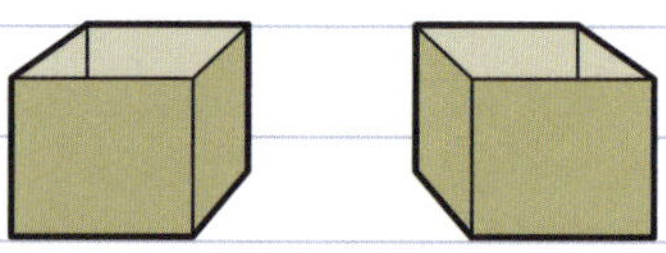

dress es

torch es

dish es

Sometimes, when a noun ends in a consonant followed by the letter **y**, such as 'lady', we take off the **y** and add the letters **ies**. Add a picture for each of these words.

one lorry

one baby

two lorries

two babies

Farm count-up

This farm is full of examples of plurals. Some follow rules and some don't. Work out the correct plurals and add word stickers to describe each set of animals.

Delightful describing

Adjectives are describing words, such as **big** and **friendly**. Some adjectives can be made by adding **y** to a noun.

Add a word sticker to describe each picture below.

To make the words below into adjectives you **double the last letter and then add y**. Look at the first one, then change the other words to adjectives. Find a picture sticker for each word.

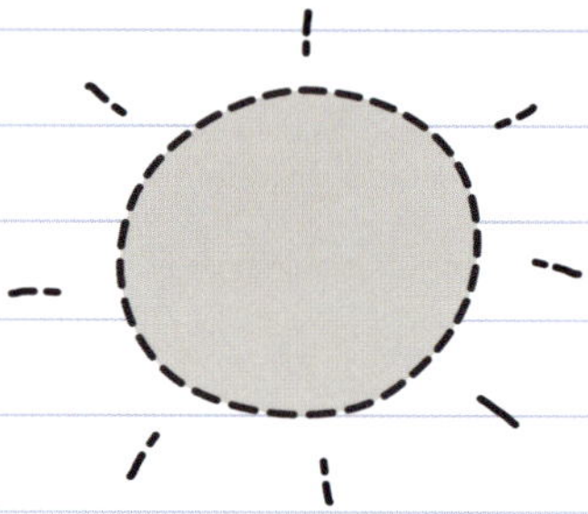

sun**ny**

mud__

spot__

If a noun ends with **e**, **take off the e and add y** to make an adjective. Write in the adjectives below. The first one has been done for you.

wave wav**y**	stone _____	slime _____	rose ____
stripe ______	nose ____	ice ___	shine _____

Weather watch

It's been a wacky week for weather!

Can you fill in the weather chart with the missing word stickers?

Adjectives tell you more about nouns. They make your sentences more interesting to read.

Monday	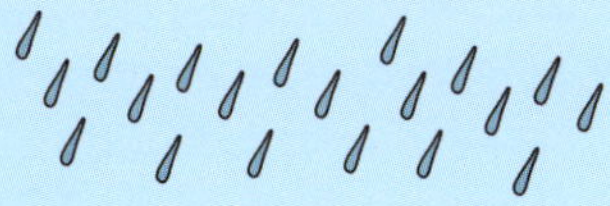	
Tuesday		
Wednesday		
Thursday		
Friday		
Saturday		
Sunday		

Sticker star time!

Weighing up words

We can add **er** or **est** to the end of many adjectives when we want to compare things:
My scarf is long, Zara's is long**er**, but Felix has the long**est** of all.

Add the missing picture sticker to finish comparing the words.

fast

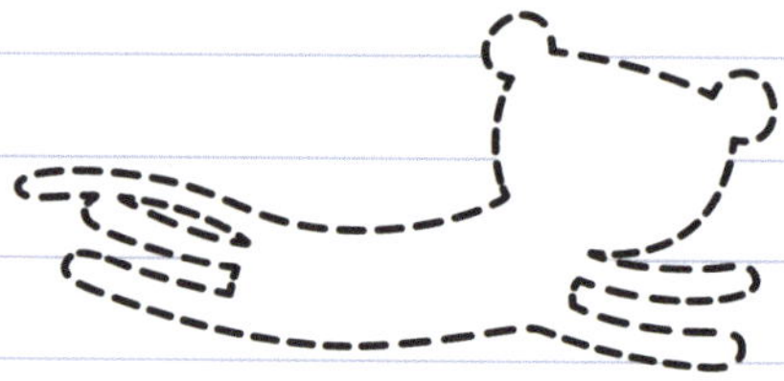
fast**er**

fast**est**

If the adjective ends in the letter **y**, change the **y** to an **i** before adding **er** or **est**:
I am happy, but Ava is happ**ier** and Jacob is happ**iest** of all.

Add the missing picture sticker below.

funny

funn**ier**

funni**est**

Park puzzle

The footballers are having fun in the park! Add the stickers to complete these sets of comparing words.

Right here, right now

We add **ing** to the end of verbs to show that something is happening now. Add a sticker to describe what each child is doing.

When a word has a **short** vowel sound (such as the sound **o** in hop) we **double the last letter before we add ing**.

Spell the **ing** words below. The first one has been done for you.

hop**ping** sit____ dig____

When the word ends in **e**, we **take off the e before we add ing**. Write the new words here. The first one has been done for you.

ride + ing = riding care + ing = ______

move + ing = ______ make + ing = ______

A trip to the circus

Write the missing action word next to each happy character.

Sticker star time!

An action or doing word is called a **verb**. When we write about things that are happening now, we are using the **present tense** of the verb.

The girl is c________ her hands.

The strongman is l______ weights.

This clown is r_____ on his unicycle.

This clown is j_______ balls.

Done and dusted

We add **ed** to the end of verbs to show that something has already happened.
Write the past tense of the verbs below.

push + ed = ______   pull + ed = ______

When the word has a short vowel sound (such as the **u** in rub) we double the last letter and add **ed**.
Write the endings to these verbs. The first has been done for you.

clapped   jog___   hop___

When the word ends in **e**, we **take off the e before we add ed**.
Write the new words here. The first one has been done for you.

like + ed = liked   race + ed = _____

smile + ed = ______   hope + ed = _____

Rowdy rulebreakers!

Some verbs change one letter or more when things have already happened.

When we write about things that have already happened, we are using the **past tense** of a verb.

For example, r**u**n becomes r**a**n.

Read this pirate's tale. Choose a verb from the list below to fill in each space.

Greetings, me hearties!

One sunset I _ _ _ another ship pass in the distance. I gave the order to raise the mainsail. The wind _ _ _ _ us there in no time. As soon as we got close by, my men _ _ _ to grab their weapons. They could tell that the ship belonged to pirates, like us!

I _ _ _ downstairs in my cabin, trying to come up with a plan. Just then there was a knock on the door. My cabin boy explained that the strange ship belonged to my brother, Old Jack Barnacles!

That night we _ _ _ a grand feast, both crews singing until the early hours.

The funniest thing about our jolly evening? My lazy parrot, George, _ _ _ _ _ through the whole party!

One-Eyed Toby

saw	**blew**	**ran**	**sat**	**ate**	**slept**

Sticker star time!

What is the opposite?

We can add **un** to the beginning of some words to make them mean the opposite:

kind unkind

Find a picture or word sticker to show the opposites below.

happy unhappy

pack unpack

tidy

Adding **dis** at the front of other words can turn them into opposites too.

like dislike

Write in the words to finish off the **dis** word sums below.

dis + **please** =

dis + **appear** =

dis + **obey** =

page 19

It's only got one **boot**.

His pupils were too **bright**.

Because it saw the tree **bark**.

A woolly **jumper**.

page 4–5

l q g w

page 7

children sheep horses

mice fish cows

page 20

witch knife

whale wreck

page 8

smelly hairy

dirty

page 23

stairs room

stairs room

shine paper

page 18

page 6

page 18

page 20

page 20

flour

page 18

blew

page 8

page 18

page 8

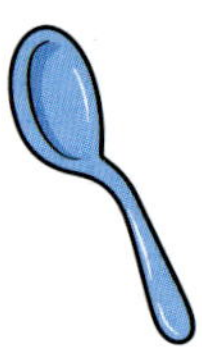

page 26

page 18

leek

page 8

page 18

sun

page 16

page 10

smaller

page 11

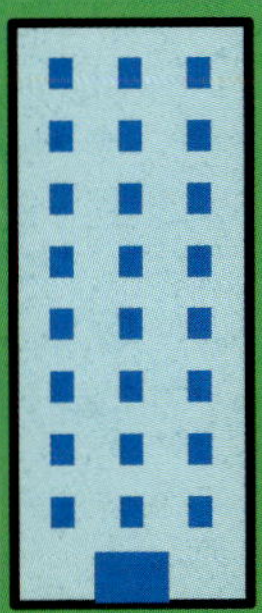

taller

highest

dirtiest

page 11

page 9

rainy

windy

cloudy

snowy

sunny

frosty

stormy

page 2

s

c

c

d

page 16

untidy

sunflower

seahorse

page 22

handbag

starfish

page 12

kicking

playing

walking

jumping

reading

looking

page 6

page 20

page 6

page 26

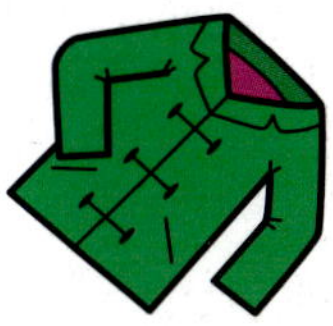

page 26

page 26

pages 24–25

All change!

Complete the sentences.

It was time for the children to get __dressed, ready for PE.

Gemma __tied her shoelaces and pulled off her hat.

Sarah __zipped her jacket and hung it on a hook.

Thomas ___liked the green T-shirt he had to wear.

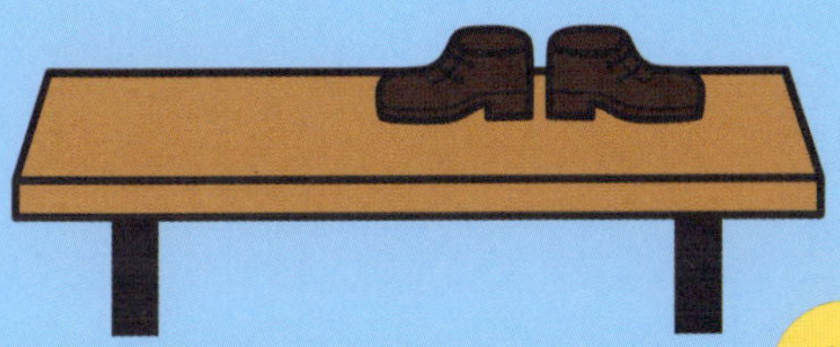

The same but different

Some words sound the same, but have a different spelling and meaning. These words are called **homophones**.

Picture pairs

Look at the words below, then add the picture stickers to sort them into pairs.

bat

ring

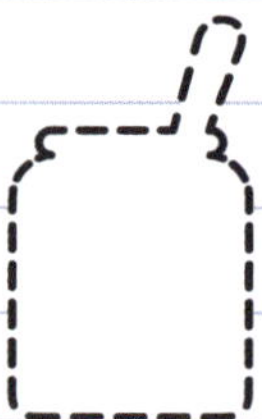

jam

Sounds like...

Add the picture stickers to sort these homophones into pairs.

Homonyms are words that sound the same and are spelt the same, but have different meanings.

Jolly jokes

A great way to learn about homonyms is to swap jokes with your friends. Stick the right funny answers to the jokes below.

What sort of dancing do plumbers like?

Why can't a car play football?

Why did the teacher wear sunglasses?

Why did the cat jump out of the tree?

What do you get if you cross a sheep with a kangaroo?

Sticker star time!

Shh! Letters in hiding

Some words contain letters that you can't hear when you say them out loud – for example, you can't hear the **w** in wrong.

Say the words and find the correct sticker.

Find the picture stickers for the words below.
Do you know which letters are silent?

guitar

knee

scissors

Funny photos!

This photo album is packed with silent letters. Write in the missing words.

The happy family group. That's me kneeling on the floor.

A sweet little _ _ _ _ .

Daisy _ _ _ _ _ _ _ along the beach.

Maria _ _ _ _ _ _ _ to her friend.

Grandad's new garden _ _ _ _ _ .

Sticker star time!

Two for the price of one

Some words can be joined with others to create a brand-new word.

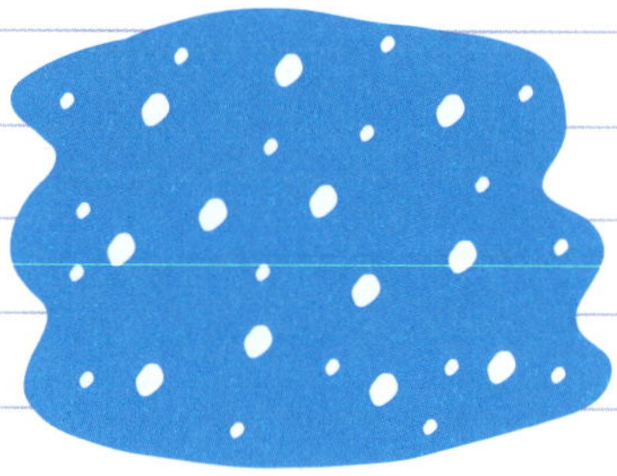 +  = 

snow man snowman

Say the new word and add in the word sticker.

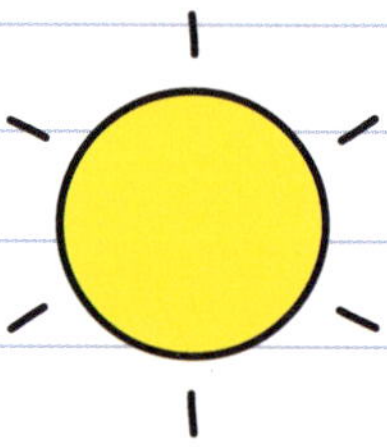 

sun + flower =

sea + horse =

hand + bag =

star + fish =

Find the compounds

Find the correct word stickers to finish off the labels on this house.

The great zoo race

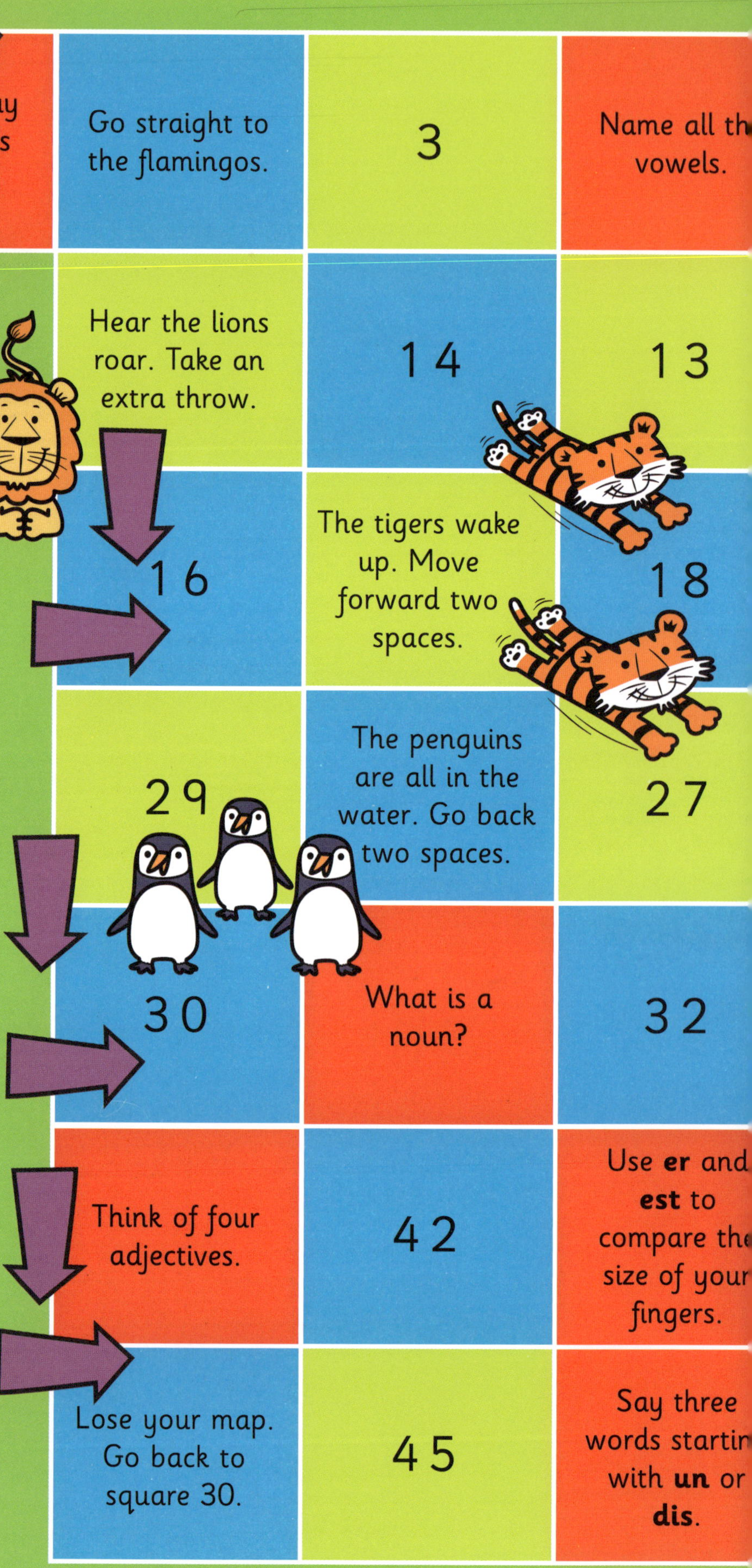

Play this game with up to three friends. Press the coloured stickers onto card and carefully cut them out. Choose a coloured counter each.

How to play

Take turns to throw a die, then move across the board as fast as you can. Follow the instructions on each square.

Each red square has a special challenge. If the others agree that it has been completed successfully, the player may move forward one extra square.

Good luck!

et lost on the way to the enguins. Miss a turn.	6	Name the 12th letter of the alphabet.	Say two words that end with 'd'.
iout out seven consonants.	1 1	Stop at the café. Miss a turn.	9
Say a letter nat completes these words: _p, h_g, p_t.	Take the zoo train to square 25.	2 1	Say three words with a long 'oo' sound in the middle.
'he reptile ouse is too usy. Miss a turn.	2 5	The giant spider doesn't scare you. Skip to square 30.	The polar bears are playing. Miss a turn.
What is the plural of 'tooth'?	3 4	It's feeding time! Go directly to square 38.	3 6
4 0	Tell a short story in the past tense.	3 8	3 7
Say two nomophones.	Take photos of the zebras. Miss a turn.	Shout out five compound words.	FINISH

Super word quiz

Rhyme time

Add a picture sticker to each word. Then, say the words and listen for the vowel sounds. Next, draw lines to match the words that rhyme.

boat **bee**

tree **spoon**

moon **coat**

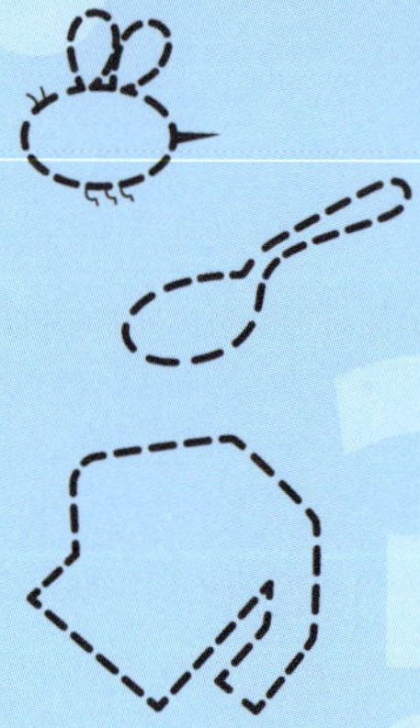

Compare the creatures

Look at the animals in each box, then circle the smallest butterfly, the biggest elephant, the hairiest bear and the stripiest tiger.

Keep your eye on the ball

There is a ball missing from each picture. Add the ball stickers, then write in the missing action word.

_ _ _ _

_ _ _

Homophone fill-in

Look at the homophones at the top of each box.
Read the words then write them in the sentence.

blew blue

She ____ up the ____ balloon.

I eye

_ have a sore ___.

sea see

He can ___ the ___.

Land ahoy!

Can you complete this spelling scene? Choose from the word list below and write the correct one above each picture.

_ _ _ _ _ _ _

_ _ _

_ _ _ _

island
waves
ship
hat
pirate
tree

_ _ _ _

_ _ _ _ _ _

_ _ _ _ _

Tricky words

Some words are quite difficult to spell and you need to learn and remember them.

Have a look at the word lists below. Cover them up and try to write them down without looking again. Put a tick next to the ones you get right.

said	______________	☐
children	______________	☐
about	______________	☐
people	______________	☐
house	______________	☐
asked	______________	☐
could	______________	☐
water	______________	☐
where	______________	☐
school	______________	☐

Look, say, cover, write, check

Here are some more tricky words for you to practise. Remember to **look** first, **say** the word, then **cover** it up while you **write** it out. **Check** to see if you were correct.

know	____________	☐
round	____________	☐
thought	____________	☐
animals	____________	☐
through	____________	☐
found	____________	☐
around	____________	☐
laughed	____________	☐
different	____________	☐
suddenly	____________	☐

Sticker star time!

Answers

Pages 2–3

Let's get started!

cap
drum
clock
spider

Happy endings

boat
umbrella
crab
shell
octopus
starfish

Pages 4–5

Jungle japes

g l q w

Short and sweet

cat
bed
pin
fox
sun
peg

A little longer

bee
flute
kite

Pages 6–7

Lots of plurals

apples
cups
boxes
dresses
torches
dishes

Farm count-up

horses
fish
sheep
cows
children
mice

Pages 8–9

Delightful describing

dirty hairy smelly
muddy spotty
stony slimy rosy
stripy nosy icy shiny

Weather watch

rainy
windy
cloudy
snowy
sunny
frosty
stormy

Pages 12–13

Right here, right now

playing
jumping
kicking
reading
walking
looking

sitting digging

caring moving making

A trip to the circus

The girl is clapping her hands.

The strongman is lifting weights.

This clown is riding on his unicycle.

This clown is juggling balls.

Pages 14–15

Done and dusted

pushed pulled

jogged hopped

raced smiled hoped

Rowdy rulebreakers!

Greetings, me hearties! One sunset I **saw** another ship pass in the distance. I gave the order to raise the mainsail. The wind **blew** us there in no time. As soon as we got close by, my men **ran** to grab their weapons. They could tell that the ship belonged to pirates, like us!

I **sat** downstairs in my cabin, trying to come up with a plan. Just then there was a knock on the door. My cabin boy explained that the strange ship belonged to my brother, Old Jack Barnacles!

That night we **ate** a grand feast, both crews singing until the early hours.
The funniest thing about our jolly evening? My lazy parrot, George, **slept** through the whole party!
One-Eyed Toby

Pages 16–17

What is the opposite?

tidy untidy
displease
disappear
disobey

All change!

It was time for the children to get undressed, ready for PE.

Gemma untied her shoelaces and pulled off her hat.

Sarah unzipped her jacket and hung it on a hook.

Thomas disliked the green T-shirt he had to wear.

Pages 18–19

Sounds like...

flower	flour
blue	blew
son	sun
leak	leek

Jolly jokes

Why can't a car play football?
It's only got one boot.

Why did the teacher wear sunglasses?
His pupils were too bright.

Why did the cat jump out of the tree?
Because it saw the tree bark.

What do you get if you cross a sheep with a kangaroo?
A woolly jumper.

Pages 20–21

Shh! Letters in hiding

knife	witch
whale	wreck

Funny photos!

lamb
walking
writing
gnome

Pages 22–23

Two for the price of one

sunflower
seahorse
handbag
starfish

Find the compounds

sunshine
upstairs
bathroom
bedroom
wallpaper
downstairs

Pages 26–27

Keep your eye on the ball

kick
hit

Homophone fill-in

She blew up the blue balloon.

I have a sore eye.

He can see the sea.

Land ahoy!

pirate
hat
tree
ship
island
waves

Reward chart

Sticker star time!

Use this chart to keep a record of your progress.

- The journey from A to Z ☆
- Letter types ☆
- Lots of plurals ☆
- Delightful describing ☆
- Weighing up words ☆
- Right here, right now ☆
- Done and dusted ☆
- What is the opposite? ☆
- The same but different ☆
- Shh! Letters in hiding ☆
- Two for the price of one ☆
- Tricky words ☆